FIT *for* TABLE

M000302778

FIT *for* TABLE

The cook's guide to game preparation field to table

Birds, Fish, large and small Game

MIKE ROBINSON
Photographs by Nick Ridley

Quiller

Copyright © 2009 Quiller Publishing Ltd

First published in the UK in 2009
by Quiller, an imprint of Quiller Publishing Ltd
Reprinted 2010, 2012

British Library Cataloguing-in-Publication Data
A catalogue record for this book
is available from the British Library

ISBN 978 1 84689 006 2

The information in this book is true and complete to the best of our knowledge. All recommendations
are made without any guarantee on the part of the Publisher, who also disclaims any liability incurred
in connection with the use of this data or specific details.

All rights reserved. No part of this book may be reproduced or transmitted in any form or by any
means, electronic or mechanical including photocopying, recording or by any information storage
and retrieval system, without permission from the Publisher in writing.

Text by Mike Robinson
Photographs by Nick Ridley unless otherwise credited
Book and cover design by Sharyn Troughton
Printed in China

Quiller
An imprint of Quiller Publishing Ltd
Wykey House, Wykey, Shrewsbury, SY4 1JA
Tel: 01939 261616 Fax: 01939 261606
E-mail: info@quillerbooks.com
Website: www.countrybooksdirect.com

CONTENTS

FOREWORD

It has been a real pleasure and honour to be involved with the production of this extremely useful book. I wish when I was starting out working with Game and Wild food that a field manual had been available to tell me concisely what to do once I had acquired my quarry. Whilst there are many techniques for processing game, these ones all work well and I hope will help aspiring game cooks to do something great with the amazing ingredients that nature provides us with. Remember, it is our duty as sportsmen and women to eat what we shoot or catch.

Mike Robinson

GAME BIRDS

PLUCKING

The basic procedure is the same for most game birds and here we have used the pheasant. Any differences between species are discussed at the end.

These photographs show examples of a number of birds both before and after plucking.

The pheasant.

Grouse.

Duck – in this case mallard.

French or red leg partridge.

Goose.

Pink-foot goose.

Prepared turkey *(photo © Copas Turkeys)*

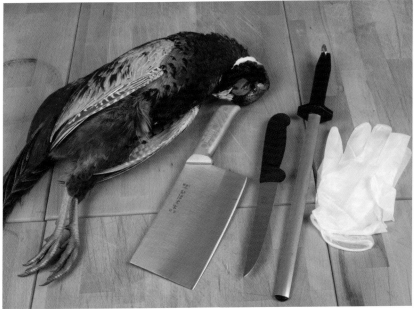

A cock pheasant and the equipment needed to deal with it. *Left to right*: cleaver, boning knife, sharpening steel, protective gloves.

Grasp the bird by its legs and wing tips. Make sure that the wing tips are folded under the bird thus exposing the bird to be plucked.

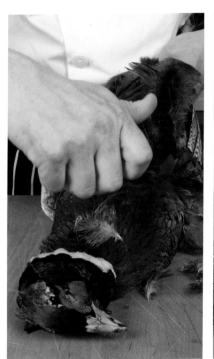

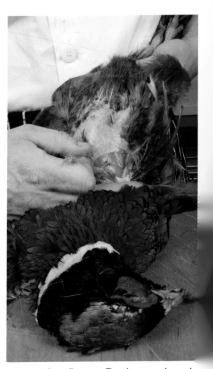

Starting from the base of the breast, grasp the feathers firmly between thumb and forefinger. Push your hand forward in short, rapid movements.

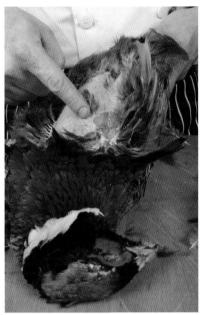
Take care not to grasp too large a bunch of feathers or the skin will tear.

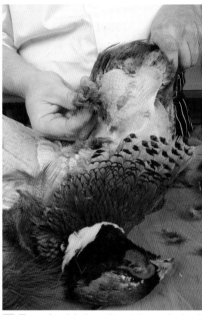
Turn the bird on its side and pluck the sides and back.

Pluck under the wings.

Using the cleaver, remove the wings at the joint as shown.

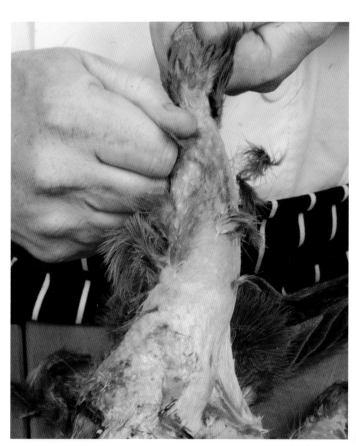

Carefully pluck the small feathers from thigh and leg – remembering always to pluck against the lie of the feather.

Pull out the tail feathers with a vigorous tug.

Remove the tail with the cleaver.

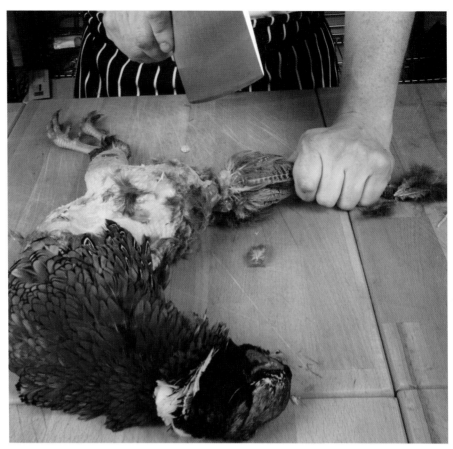

Pluck the neck and then remove the head at the base of neck.

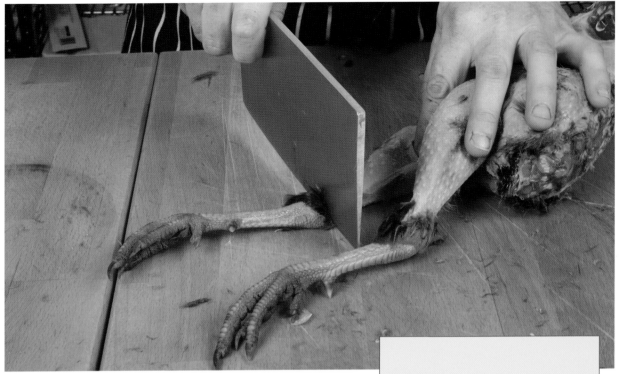

Using a cleaver, remove the legs at the knee joints.

Geese and ducks have very downy under feathers and these can be removed with a blow torch.

A blow torch will remove any remaining downy feathers.

The bird is now ready to be drawn.

Plucking woodcock

Pluck with the head on and do not remove the legs.

1 Plucking the head

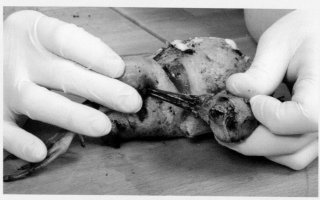

2 Push the beak through the leg joints.

3 Completely plucked bird with butter on breasts.

4 Oven-ready and with bacon covering breasts.

English partridge

As with the woodcock, the legs should be left on.

SKINNING

The information given here is identical for all birds. In this sequence we have again used a pheasant.

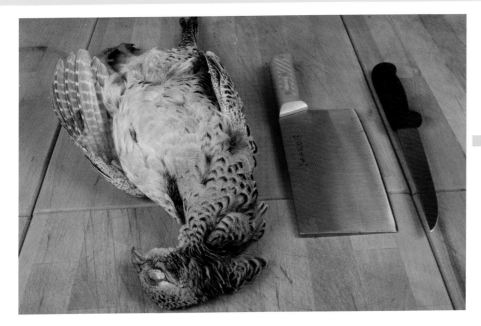

The tools needed. *Left to right*: cleaver, boning knife.

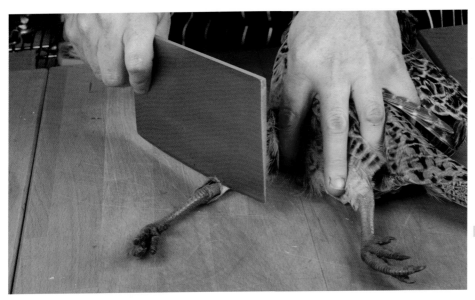

Grasp the bird firmly. Using the cleaver, remove legs at the knee joint and wings from the body.

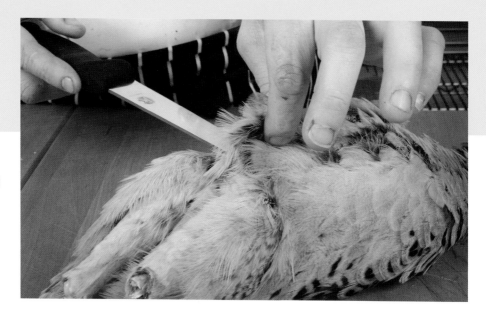

Push the skin up between the thighs and make a small cut and then lay the bird on its back with the head facing away from you.

Put your thumbs into the incision, tearing the skin open.

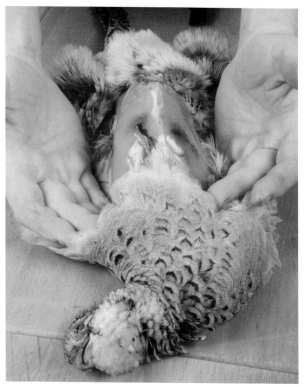

Push the skin back using the flat of your hands facing towards the table top. The breasts are now fully exposed.

To skin the legs, push the skin downwards and forwards as shown. Repeat on the other side.

Separate the tail from the body.

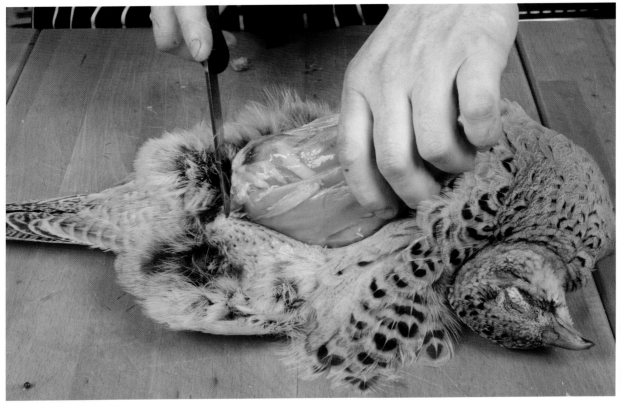

Grasp the skin firmly with one hand and legs and thighs with the other. Pull apart smartly.

Cut off the head at base of the neck.

The skinned bird.

BREASTING

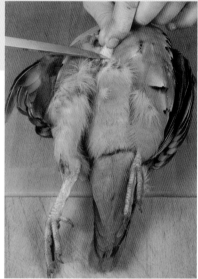

With a boning knife, make a small incision at the skin around the breast bone.

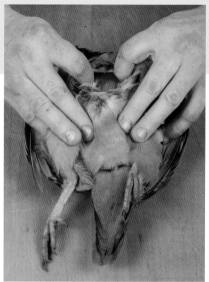

Insert your thumbs in the incision and tear the skin apart along the breast bone.

With the sides of your hands push the skin down and away from the breasts as far as possible towards the wing bases.

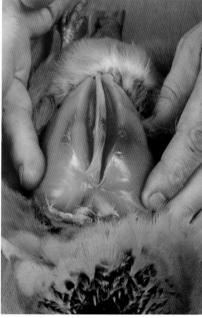

With a sharp boning knife make a single cut either side of the breast bone as shown in these photographs.

Run the knife from the head end of either incision following the wish bone towards the wing root. Pulling the exposed flesh away from the rib cage, remove from the carcass. Repeat on the other side.

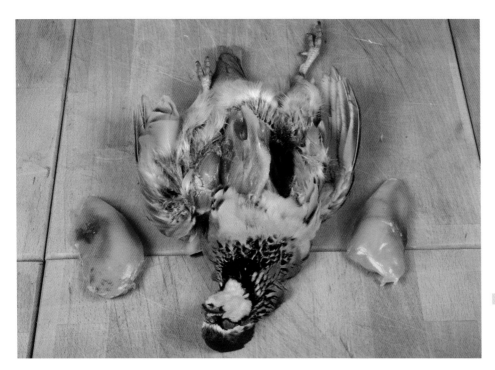

The end result.

It is unusual to take the breasts off a grouse unless the bird is damaged.

These photographs illustrate the difference in meat colour between grouse (*left*) and French partridge.

A frequently asked question at my cookery school is how do you tell the difference between old and young grouse. The way to do this is to hook your forefinger under the bird's beak and then place the ball of your thumb on its skull between the eyes. Press firmly – with a young bird the skull will give way under pressure.

CROWNING

If you want to cook the breast of a bird or to bone it then it is often a good idea to remove the crown. This is easily achieved by starting with a plucked bird as shown.

 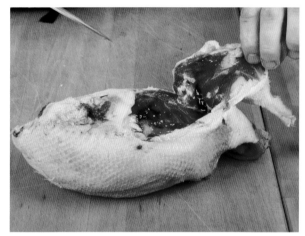

First remove the legs.

Lay the carcass flat and cut diagonally from the back end to the centre of the back just underneath the rib cage. Do this on both sides.

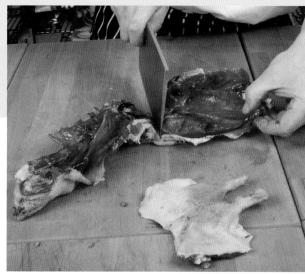

▓ Using a cleaver, cut through at the wing joints.

▓ The end result.

GUTTING OR DRAWING

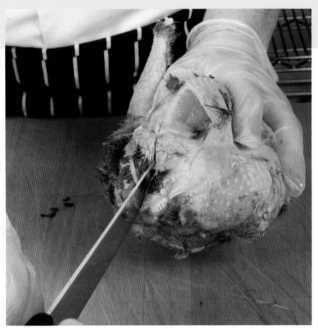

Make a vertical cut down through the anal vent.

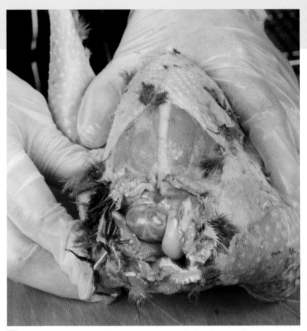

Push down on the bird to push its innards towards the incision.

Insert two fingers.

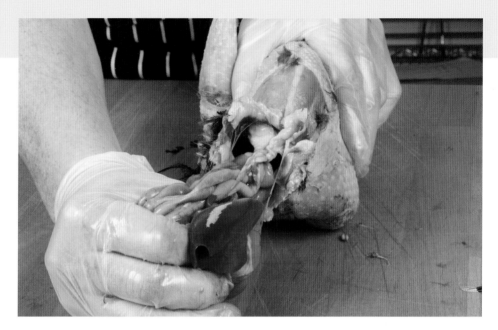

▐ Grasp the innards.

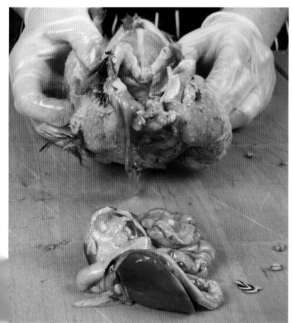

▐ Pull the innards out in one movement.

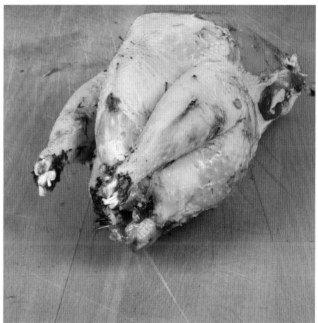

▐ The gutted bird.

Pigeon

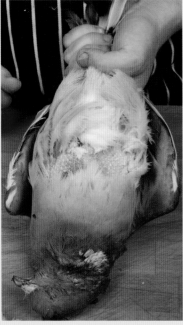

1 Prepare as described for other birds. However as pigeon feathers will go everywhere many people prefer only to pluck the breasts instead of plucking the whole bird.

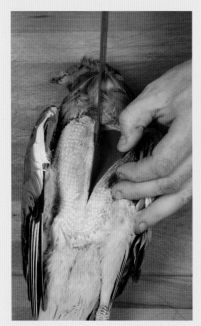

2 Slice down either side of breast bone to remove breasts.

3 This is done as with any other bird as seen here.

DEER

BLEEDING AND GRALLOCHING

The deer used to illustrate this chapter is a Sika pricket (eighteen month old male).

Important note:

All hunters must inspect the pluck of the animal in accordance with best practice guidelines as taught in the Deer Stalking Certificate qualifications. This is a legal requirement for any deer entering the food chain.

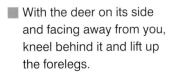 Once the deer has been shot and located I always ensure that it is properly dead. I do this by touching the muzzle of my rifle to its eyeball and checking that it does not blink.

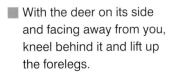 With the deer on its side and facing away from you, kneel behind it and lift up the forelegs.

Wearing protective gloves, locate the hollow notch at the front end of the breastbone, insert a sharp knife to a depth of 3 or 4 inches (76 to 102cm). Push the knife in and wriggle it to ensure that the major blood vessels around the heart are severed. 'Unzip' the neck. Cut the skin to the chin and run the knife along the opening as far as oesophagus.

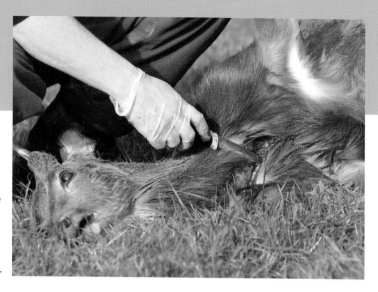

Lay the carcass on its back. Spread out the hind legs and stand with a foot on each hind leg to brace it, leaving you with both hands free to work on the carcass. As this is a male deer, grasp the penis and pull upwards away from the deer's belly and make a cut as shown here.

Cut down either side of the skin, taking care not to puncture the guts.

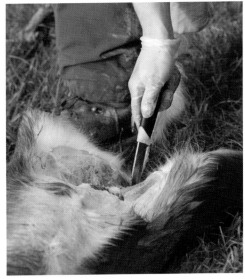

■ Continue cutting the skin down towards the anus as far as possible.

■ Now change position. Fold back the hind legs into the deer's stomach (as shown). Hold the legs in place with your left knee (leaving both hands free to work).

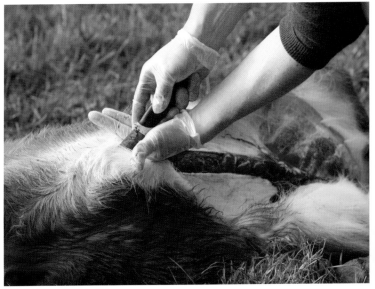

■ Resume your earlier position (i.e. with a foot on each hind leg). At the base of the belly make a small (approximately 1 inch or 25cm) shallow incision just sufficient to cut through the membrane without puncturing the gut itself.

■ Cut cleanly around the anal vent to free up the sphincter. Ensure this is completely free to allow for easy removal.

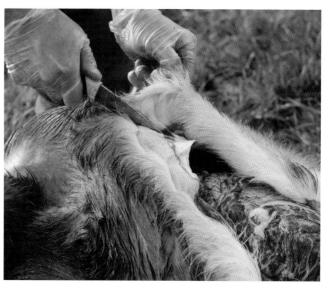

■ Place the knife with the blade up between two fingers (i.e. using the fingers as a guide) and make an incision up towards the notch at the beginning of the breastbone.

■ Continue to cut from the existing cut to the previous one made in the neck. Saw open the chest along the centre of the breastbone.

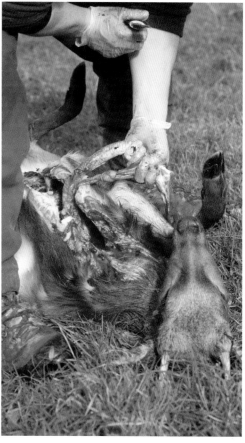

■ Separate the trachea from the oesophagus. Cut the oesophagus as high up the neck as possible and tie in a knot to prevent carcass contamination. Reach inside and pull the anus through. Lay the deer on its side, cut the diaphragm on either side and pull the gralloch out using the knife to release it where necessary.

LARDER PREPARATION

Once the deer has been bled, it should be left to hang and cool for twenty-four hours. When done commercially this will be in a refrigerated larder.

■ First remove the back legs. If you follow this sequence it will be evident how this is done. On the outside of the deer's leg locate the point between the scent gland and knuckle. The first cut is made exactly between these two points, severing the tendons and going into the joint. When the leg is sharply bent in the direction away from the cut the leg will break cleanly and can be removed.

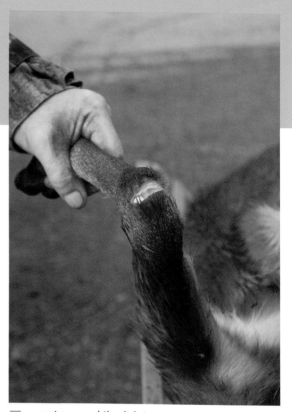

■ For the front legs, simply bend the leg at the knee joint …

■ … cut around the joint …

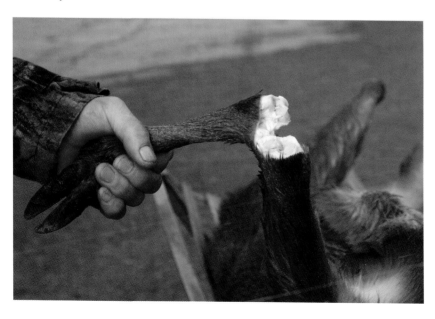

■ … then twist and turn sharply to break.

■ To remove the head, pull the deer hard by one ear towards you.

■ Then make a cut into the back of the neck at the base of the skull.

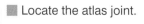 Locate the atlas joint.

Keep pulling from the ear and cut until the atlas joint and the head will come off readily.

The deer is now ready for skinning.

SKINNING

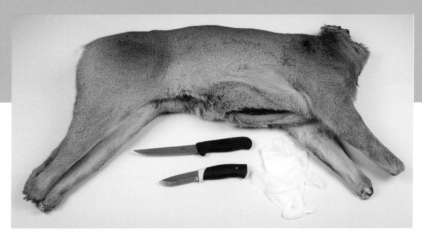

■ Skinning knife *(top)* and butchering knife *(bottom)*.

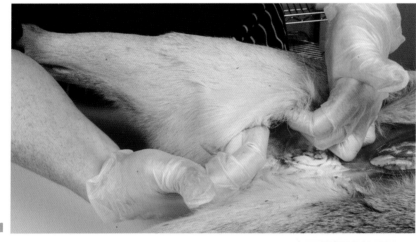

1

■ Separate the skin from the inner thigh.

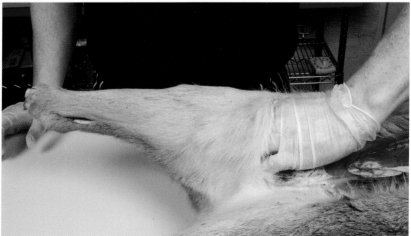

2

1

■ Cut upwards the length of the leg through the skin.

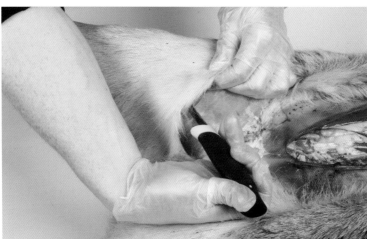

2

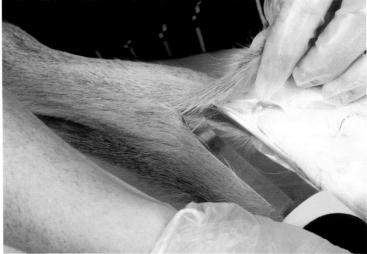

3

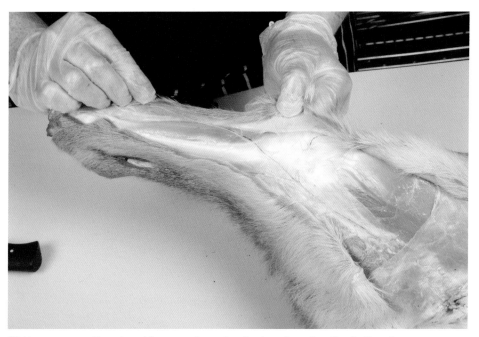

Now start pulling the skin away from the flesh only using the knife when necessary.

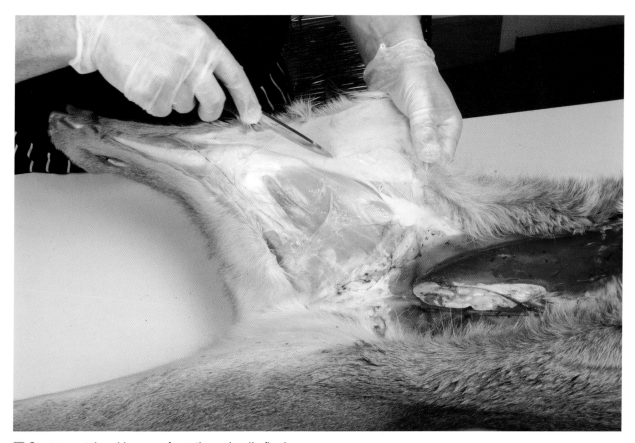

Start to cut the skin away from the animal's flanks.

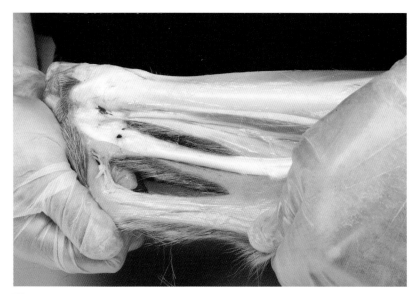

■ Carefully cut the skin around the Achilles tendon making sure not to cut the tendon itself.

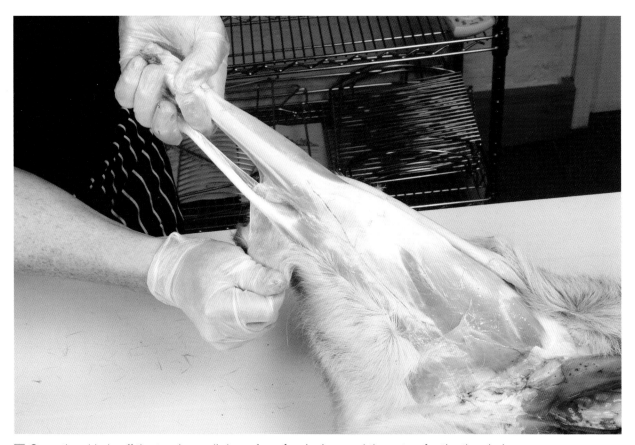

■ Once the skin is off the tendon pull down for a few inches and then stop for the time being.

■ There is a flap of meat that runs from the thigh along the flanks of the animal that is firmly attached to the skin. At this stage you need to cut behind this and free it up otherwise it will remain attached when the skin is removed.

1

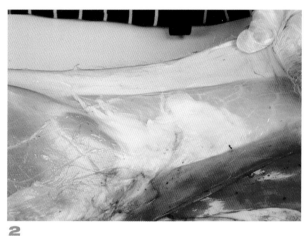

2

3

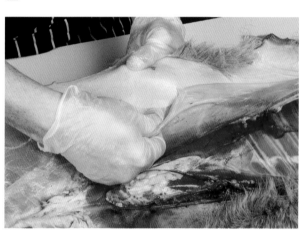

4

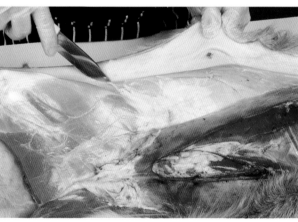

5

Skin both flanks and both hind legs.

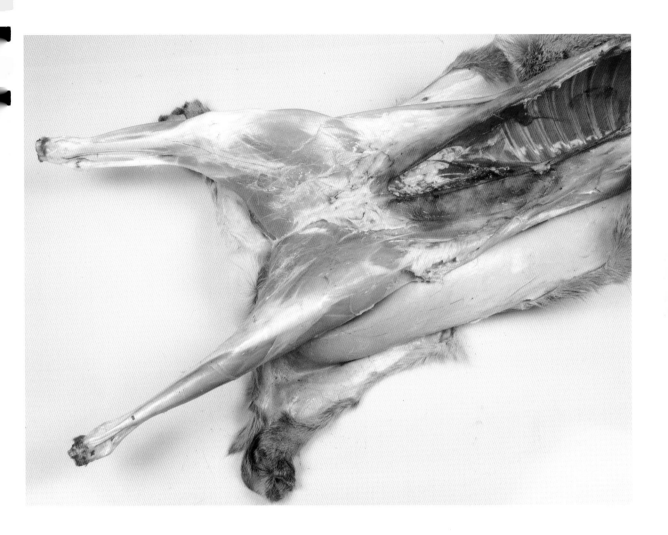

■ Hang the carcass from the Achilles tendon ensuring it is secure.

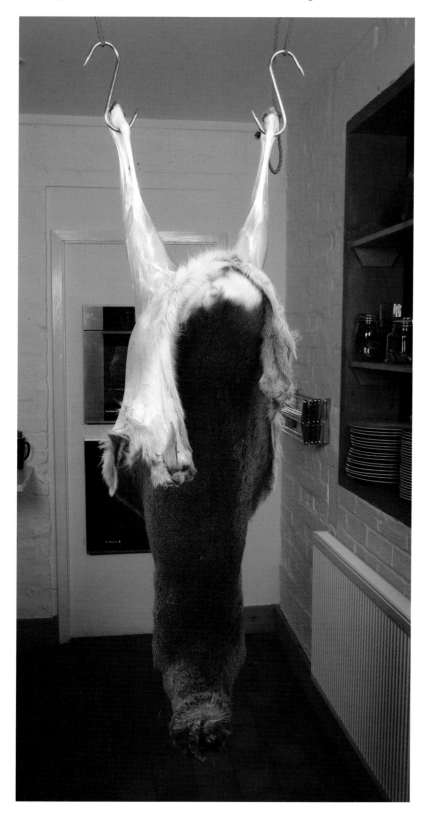

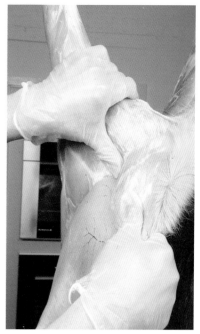

■ Work the skin away from the meat carefully.

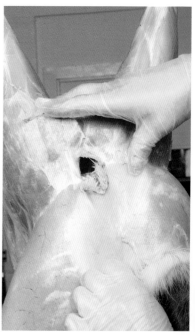

■ Work around the rear end.

Keep removing the skin using your hands, making sure that none of the meat comes off with the skin.

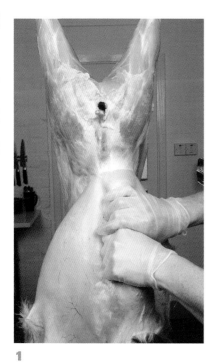

1

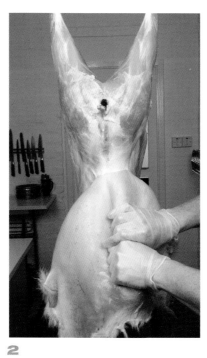

2

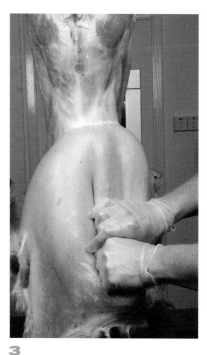

3

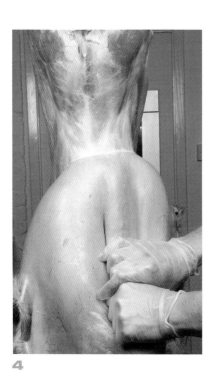

4

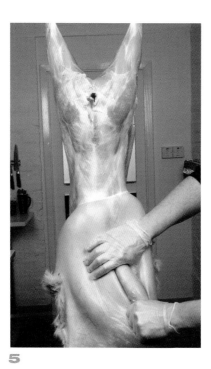

5

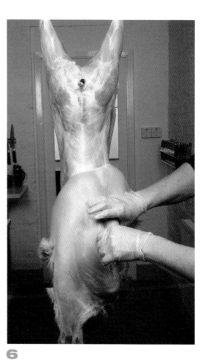

6

When you come to the shoulders roll the skin off the legs as seen here.

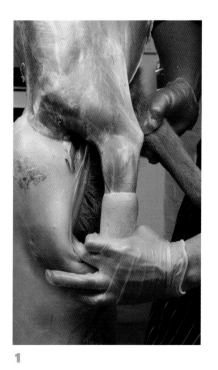

1

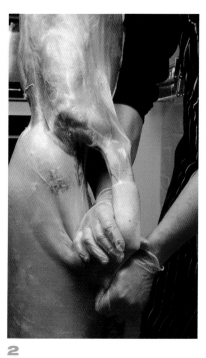

2

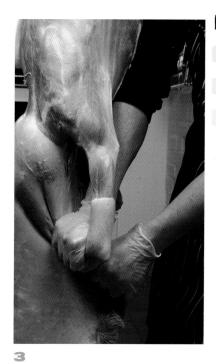

3

4

5

6

■ Finally pull the skin off the neck.

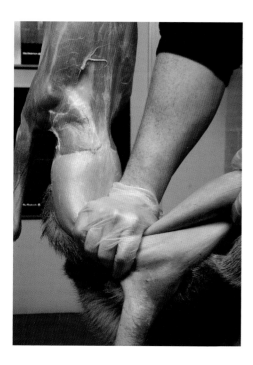

■ The skinned carcass.

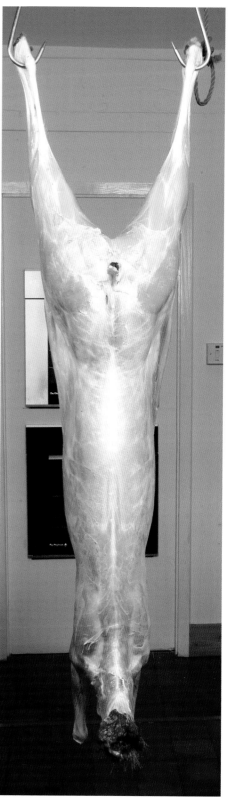

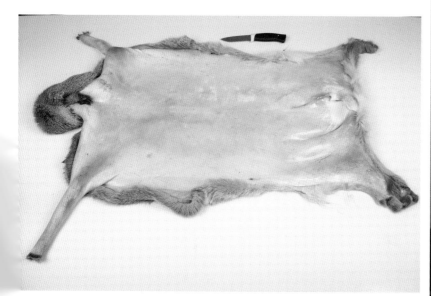

■ How a skin should look.

BUTCHERING

Lift the shoulder and cut out underneath to remove in one piece.

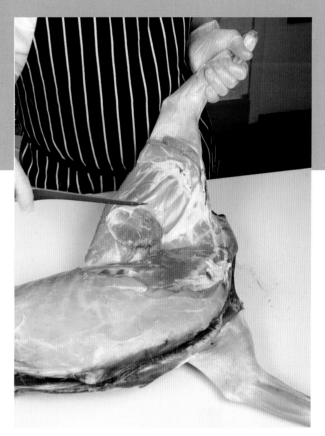

There is no ball and socket joint in the shoulder – it is completely free floating.

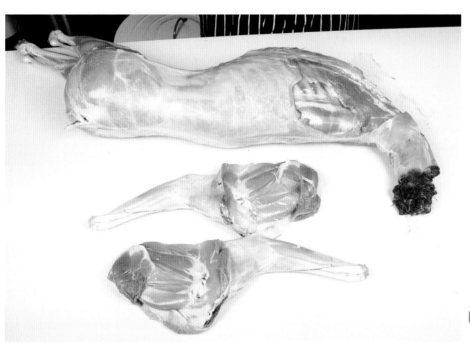

Carcass with shoulder removed.

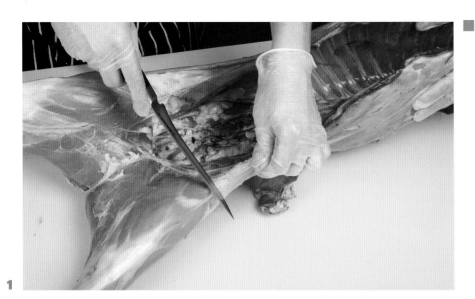

1

2

3

■ Carcass with flanks removed.

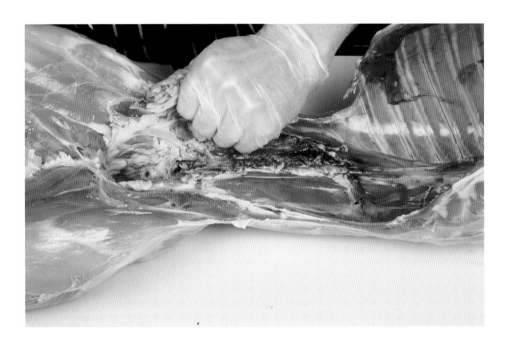

■ Remove any excess fat from around the tenderloins.

Next, carefully remove the tenderloins.

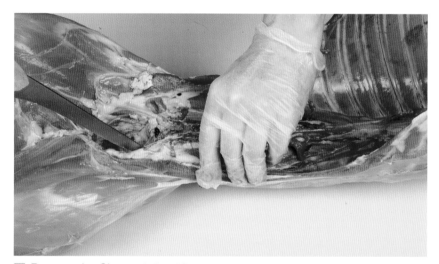

Remove the Chateaubriand from inside the thigh…

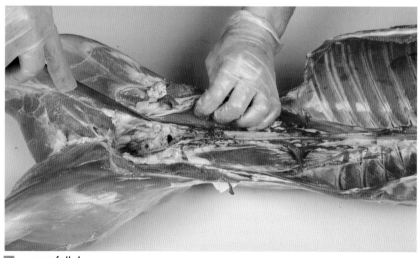

…carefully!

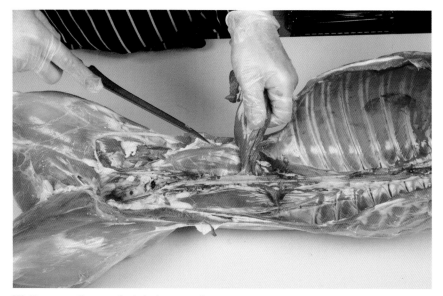

Remove the tenderloin in one piece.

Removed tenderloin.

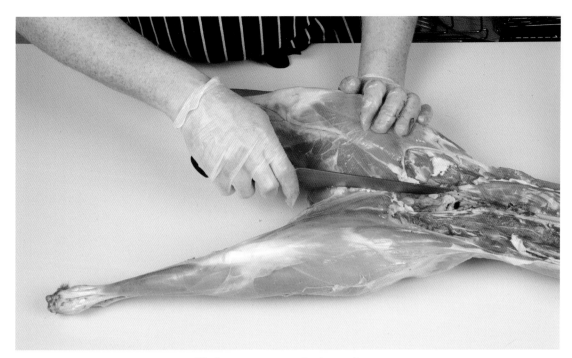

■ Start to remove the haunches.

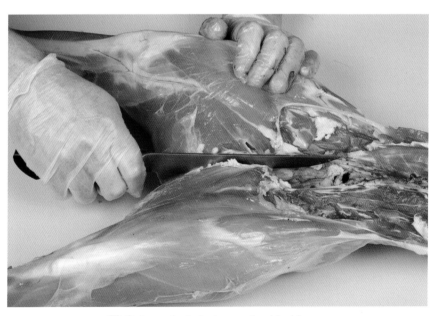

■ Cut precisely between the hind legs.

■ Make a deep incision and cut as shown in this series of photographs.

1

2

3

4

5

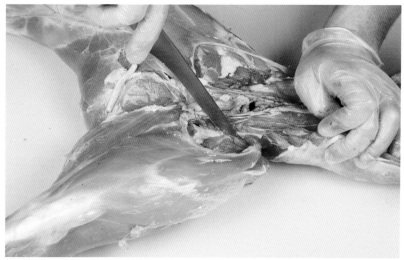

■ Turn the carcass on its back and continue to cut down inside the thigh…

■ …until you find the ball and socket joint in the hip.

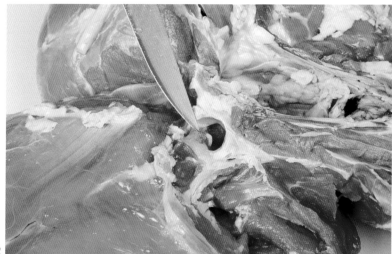

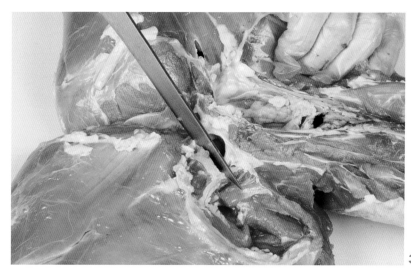

■ Cut the tendon around the socket joint.

Follow the bone of the pelvis until you join up with the outside cut…

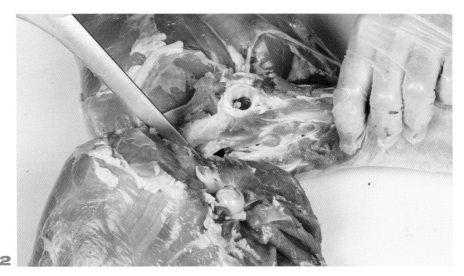

…and the haunch comes away. Repeat on the other side.

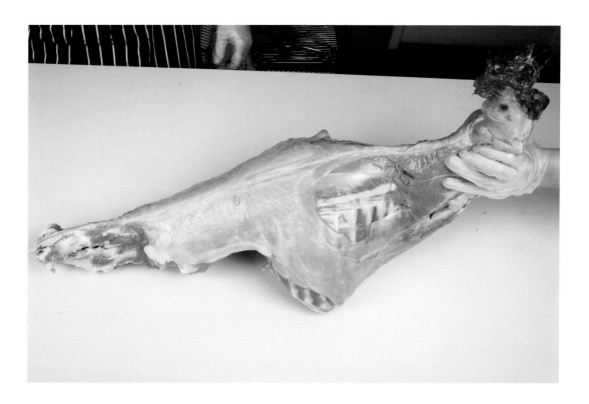

■ Lay the carcass on its front and cut from neck to pelvis along either side of the backbone.

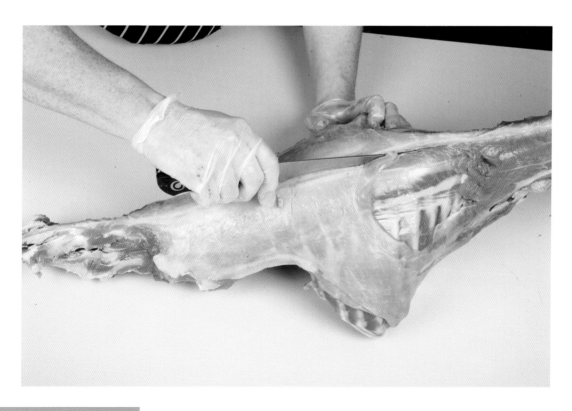

Cut above wing of the pelvis to join up with lengthways cut you have just made.

Carefully cut loin off ribs.

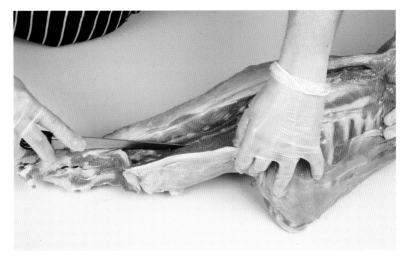

Make sure no meat is left on the bone.

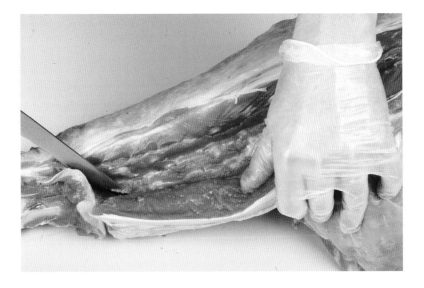

■ The loins ready for removal from the carcass.

■ Cut at the neck to release.

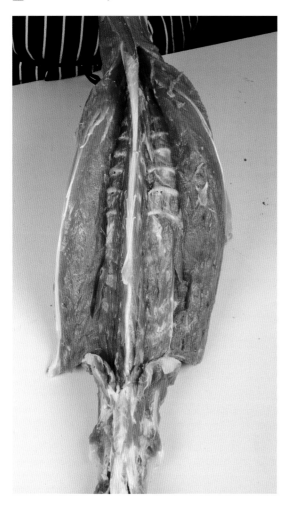

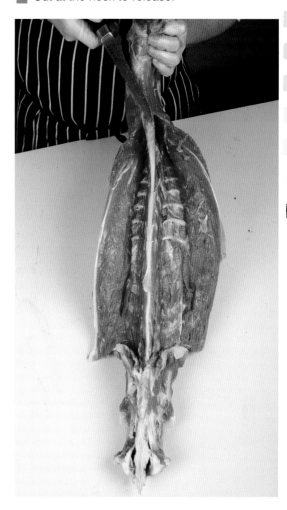

■ Take any remaining meat off the ribs and neck.

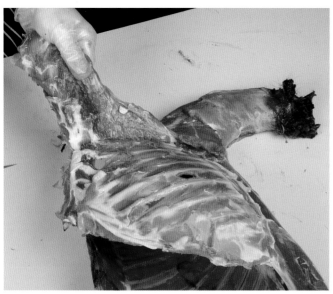

1

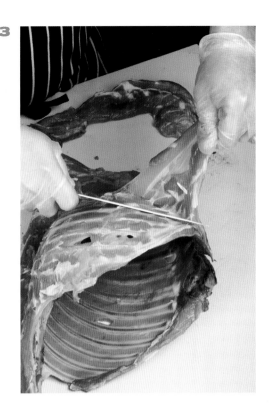

The jointed carcass.

Removing sinew

It is important that all sinew is removed from the venison.

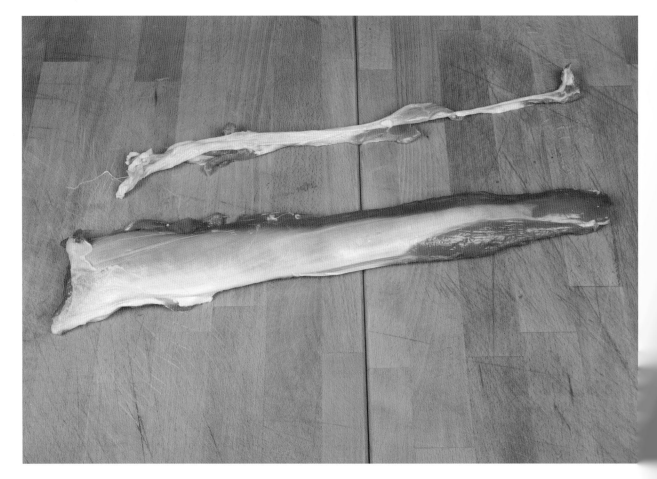

■ To do this, insert a knife between sinew and venison and gently cut away.

■ The sinew-free venison ready for cooking.

Turning haunch into steaks

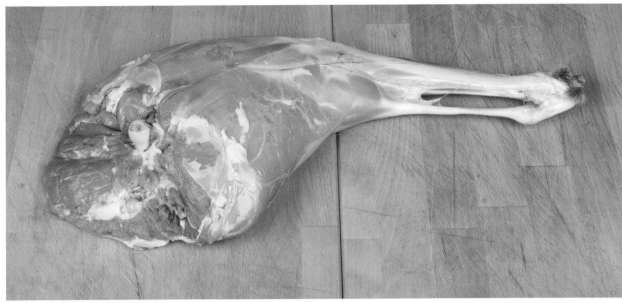

Remove the Achilles tendon.

Cut along the length of the thigh bone

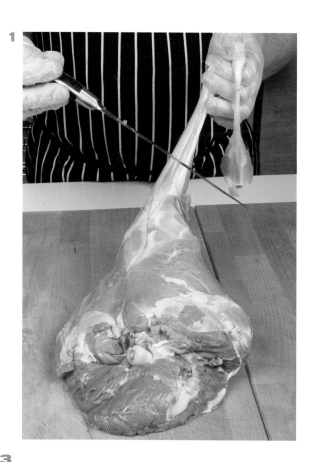

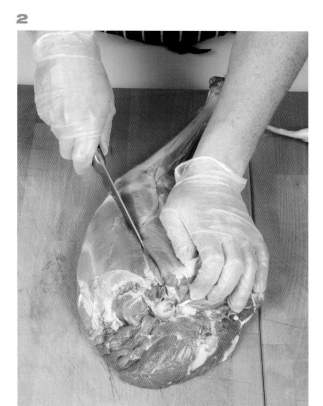

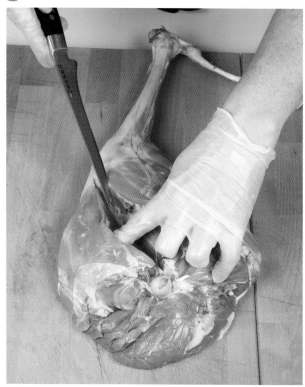

■ Remove the bone as neatly as possible.

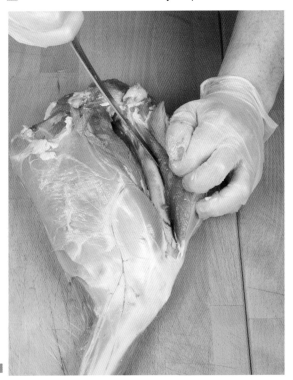

1

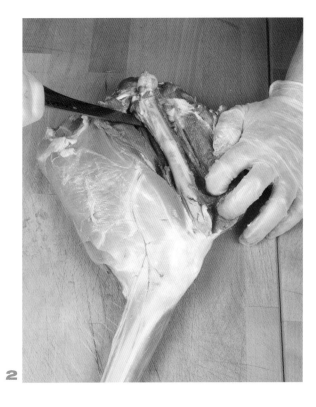

2

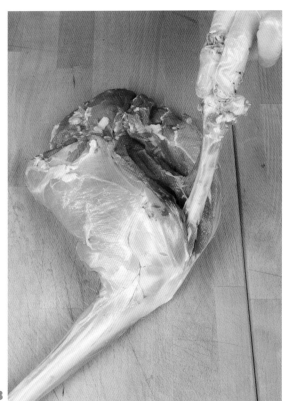

3

■ Continue cutting down the side of the shin bone.

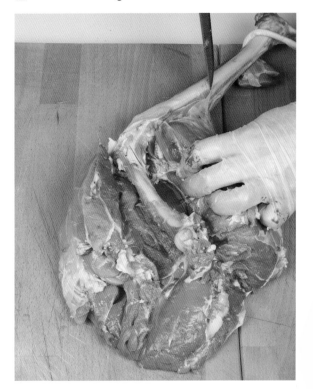

■ Finally take both bones out in one piece.

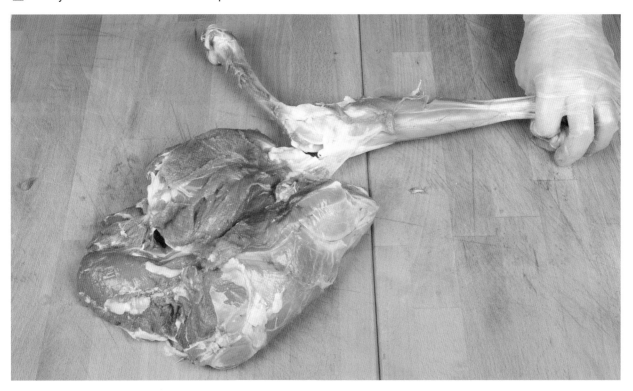

■ The boned-out haunch.

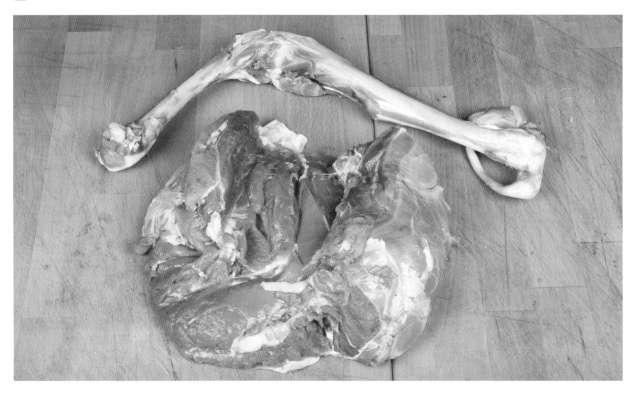

To break up the haunch

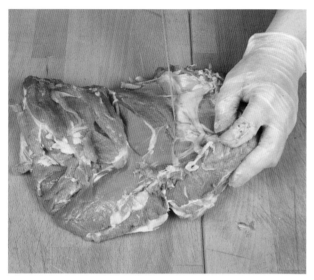

■ Start to pull the main primal muscles apart.

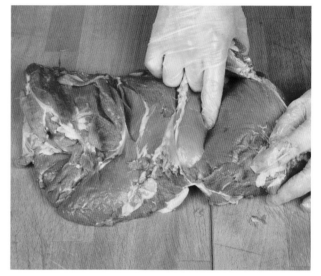

■ Pull the primals apart with your hands.

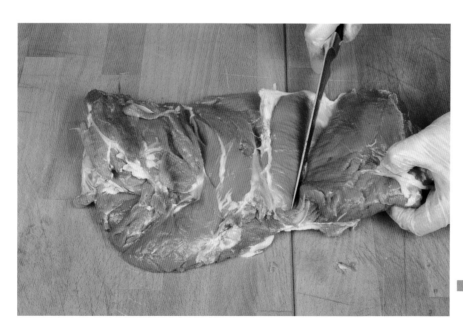

■ Cut through the sinew that connects them.

The broken up haunch.

Trim all sinew from the primal muscles.

To remove the sinew effectively, push a thin-bladed knife between flesh and sinew and remove carefully.

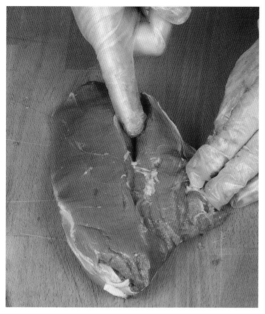

■ This primal muscle breaks down into two more pieces as shown.

■ When fully trimmed, these primals produce an amazing venison steak.

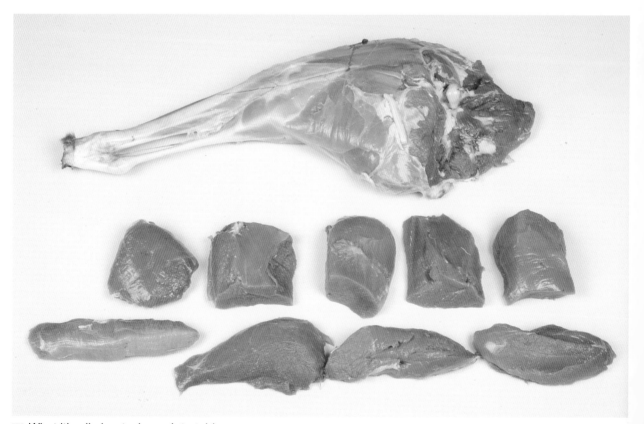

■ What it's all about – haunch to table.

BOAR

GUTTING

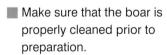 Back from hunting.

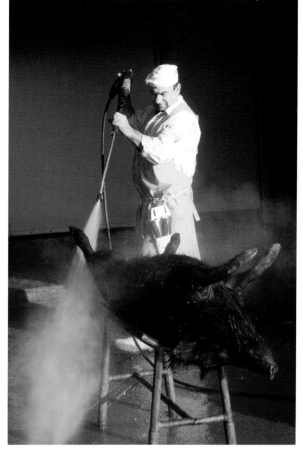

Make sure that the boar is properly cleaned prior to preparation.

■ Lay the boar on a cradle or similar surface.

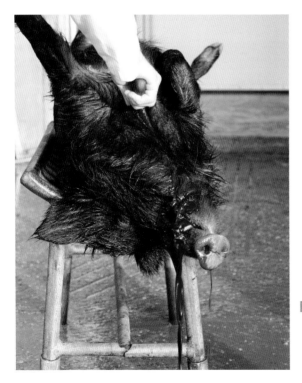

■ Push the knife into the chest cavity via the notch at the base of its throat.

■ Cut along the animal's neck – this will bleed the carcass.

■ Make a quick line cut along the breastbone…

■ finally cutting down to the breastbone itself.

1

2

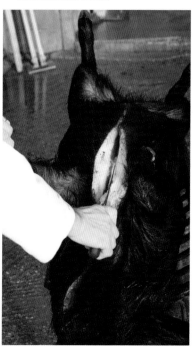

3

■ Remove the legs by cutting through the joints.

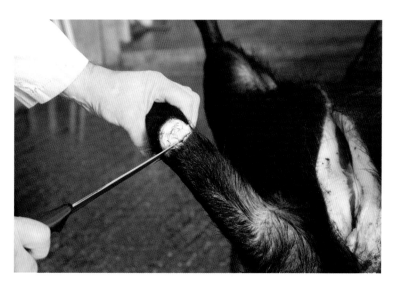

1

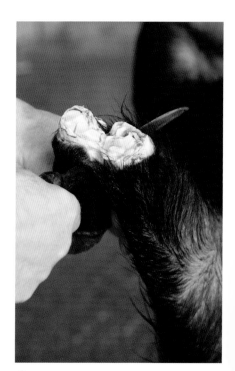

2

■ Do the same for the hind legs (as described for a deer on page 36).

■ Continue to cut using a butcher's saw and cut through the breastbone.

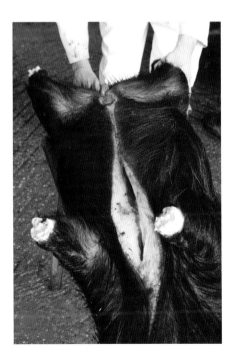 

■ Cut from the breastbone to the groin to expose the viscera.

■ Continue this cut to the anus.

■ Cut all around the sphincter.

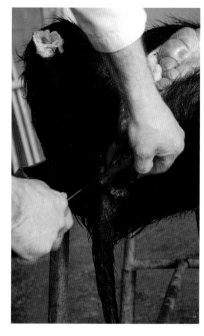

■ Hang the boar by its hind legs. To do this, make a cut behind each Achilles tendon to make a hanging point.

■ Reach up inside the animal and pull the rectum and anus through and out.

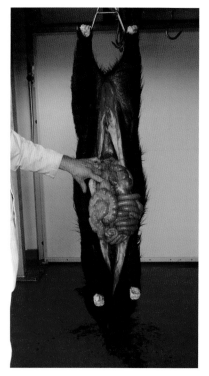

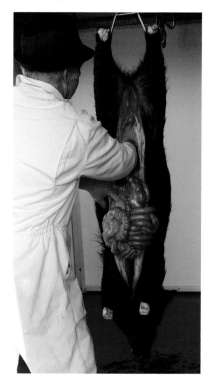

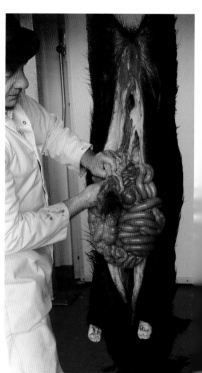

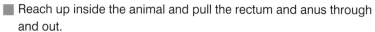

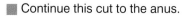

■ Start pulling the viscera down and out of the carcass using the knife to separate the diaphragm.

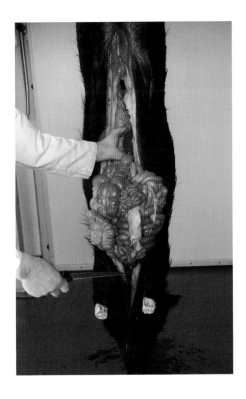

■ The carcass will be left with the trachea and oesophagus still attached; pull down as far as possible and remove.

■ Examine the viscera for any abnormalities.

SKINNING

Skinning a boar is unlike skinning a deer in that there is no membrane between the skin and the flesh and the skin has to be flayed from a boar.

■Start with the knife working the skin away from the flesh on one side.

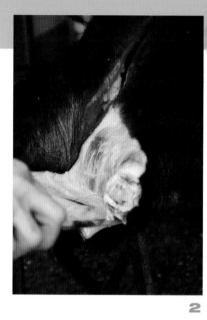

1

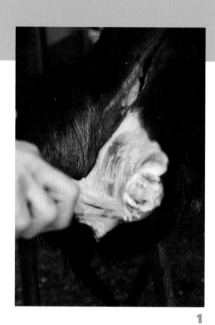

2

3

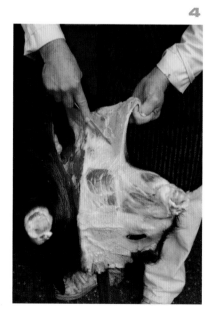

4

5

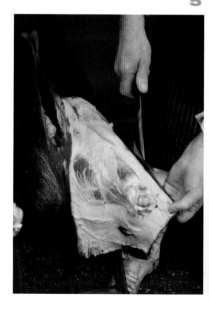

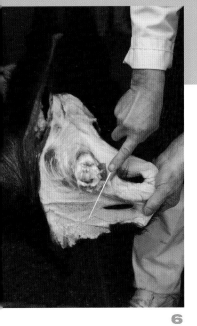

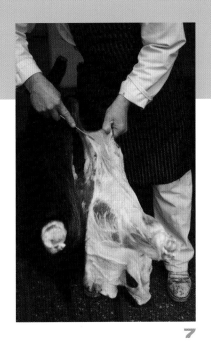

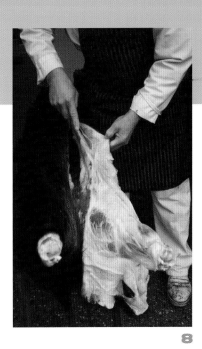

6

7

8

9

10

11

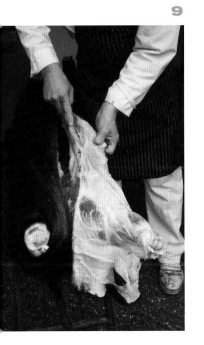

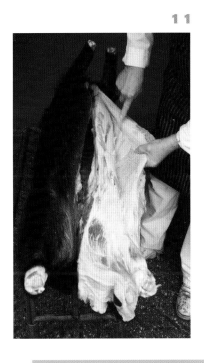

■ Working up the flanks to the front legs.

■ The skin is now removed from one side – repeat the process on the other.

■ Stop the process once you get to a half skinned carcass and then hang by its legs.

■ Once hung up, the remainder of the skin can be steadily removed as far as the neck.

1

2

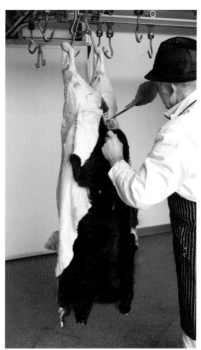

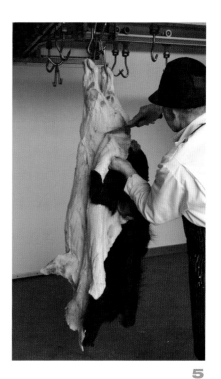

3

4

5

6

7

8

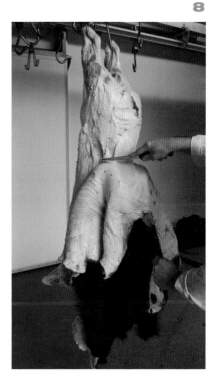

■ Once you have skinned as far as the neck, sever the head by cutting through the Atlas joint.

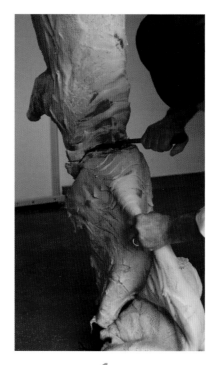

1

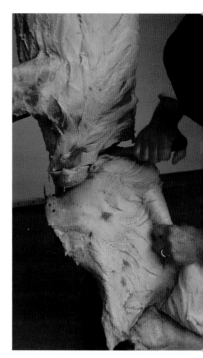

2

3

4

5

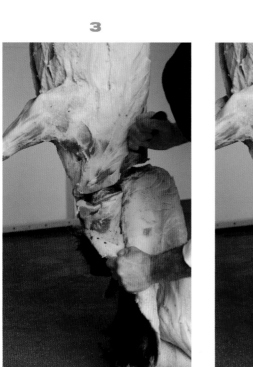

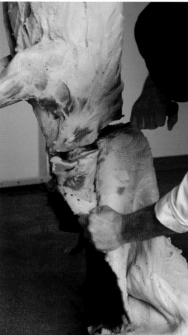

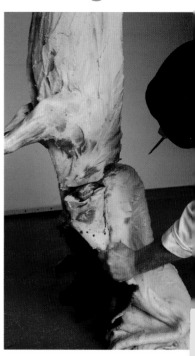

6

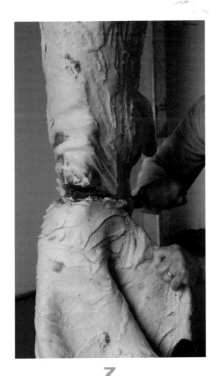

7

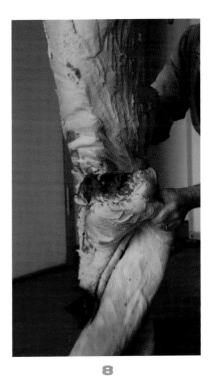

8

9

10

11

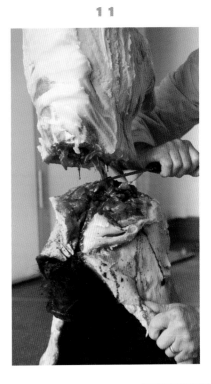

BUTCHERING

Lay the boar on its back on a butcher's block or work surface and start by cutting behind the shoulder. Then cut inside the shoulder and around to release the joint on one piece as shown. Do this on both sides.

1

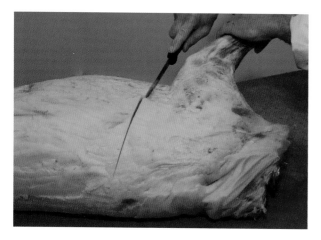

2

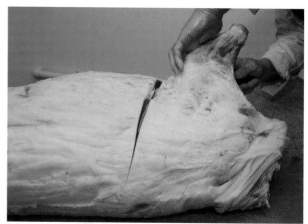

3

4

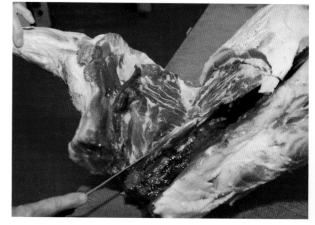

5

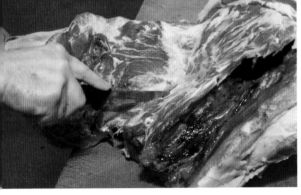

6

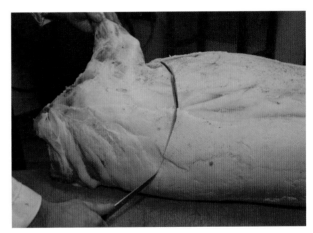

7

8

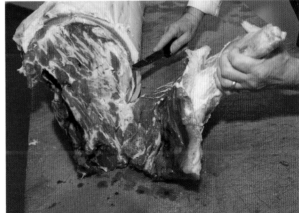

■ Make a cut in front of the haunch on the side and…

■ …take it to a half way point as shown in the photograph and up to the first rib.

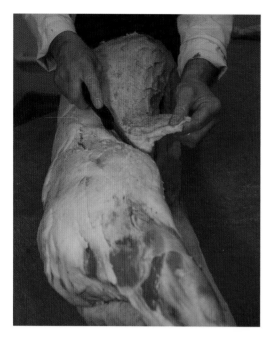

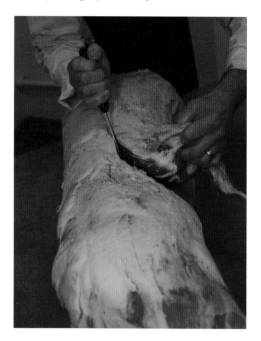

■ Make a guideline cut half way along the length of the ribs.

■ Saw off the ribs and repeat on the other side.

■ Using a saw, remove the neck.

■ The saddle and haunches are now left.

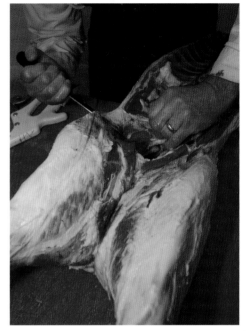

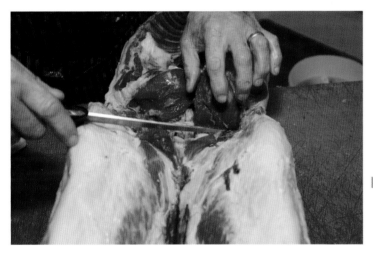

■ Remove the thick end of the tenderloin from the inner haunch.

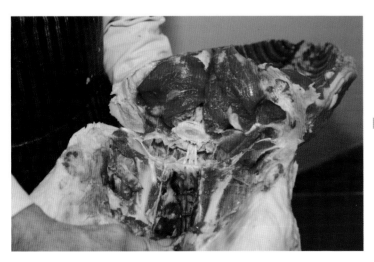

■ Locate the joint in the spine and bend backwards and break. Remove haunches from saddle.

Carefully remove both haunches from the H-bone (pelvic girdle). To do this, use the knife and follow the bones of the pelvis. Cut the ball and socket joint in the hip and remove the haunch from the bone.

1

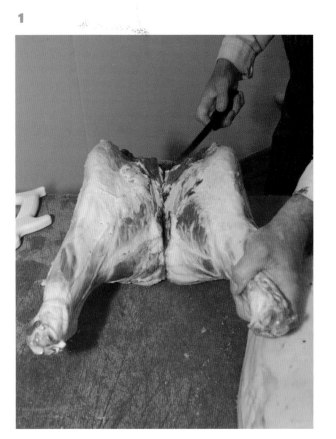

2

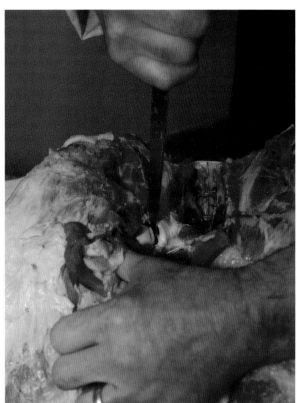

3

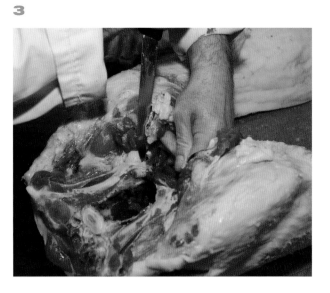

4

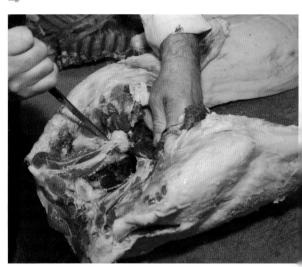

5

6

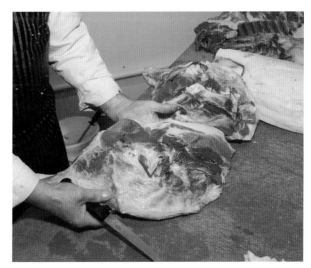

7

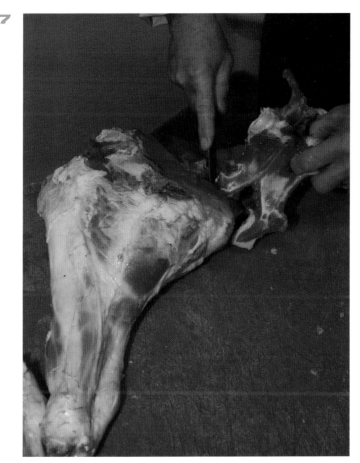

■ The broken up boar – shoulders, haunches, flanks and saddle.

RABBIT
AND OTHER SMALL GAME

PAUNCHING

The information described is suitable for all small, furred game – rabbit, squirrel, hare.

Boning knife *(top)* and sharpening steel.

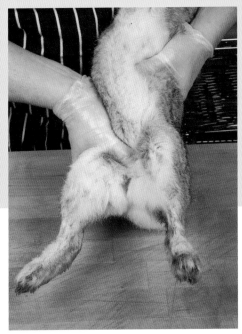

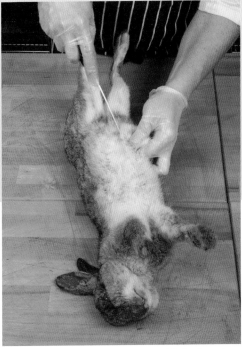

Hold the rabbit facing away from you and run your thumb down its belly to ensure that its belly is empty.

Lay the rabbit on its back with its head away from you. Using a sharp knife, make an incision in its belly.

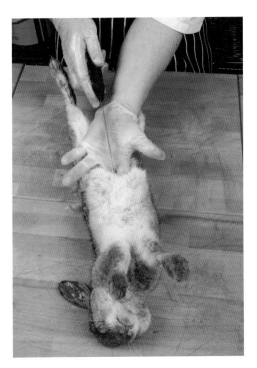

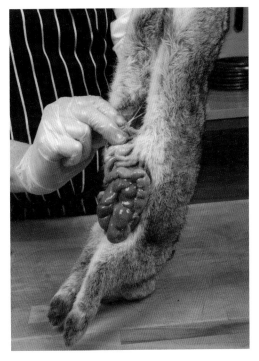

Using your fingers as a guide to prevent puncturing the gut, open the rabbit to the base of its rib cage.

Hold it by the hind legs vertically and using two fingers, remove all the guts as far as the diaphragm.

SKINNING

Separate the flanks from the skin on either side.

Using a cleaver, remove the rear and front legs at the joints.

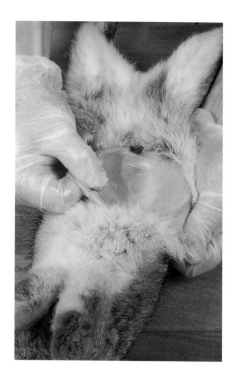

1

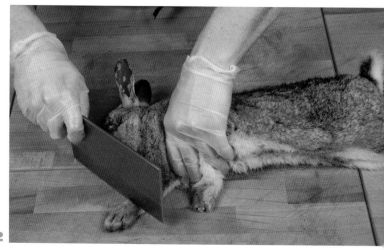

2

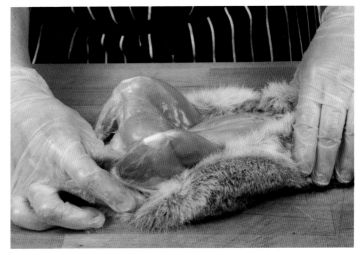

Work the skin over the hind legs of the rabbit…

…until you can cut it off at the tail as seen here.

Grasping the partially skinned rabbit by its hips, pull the skin away from the rabbit firmly until it stops at the head and shoulders.

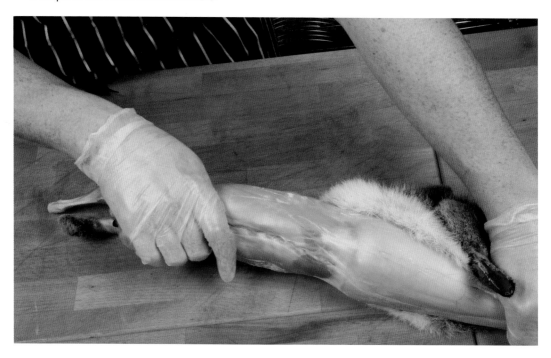

Pull the front legs away from the skin.

Chop off the head.

The rabbit is now ready for butchering.

BUTCHERING

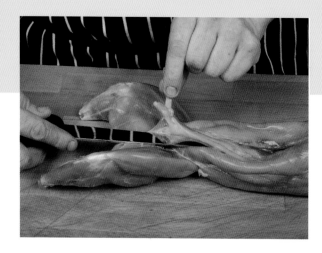

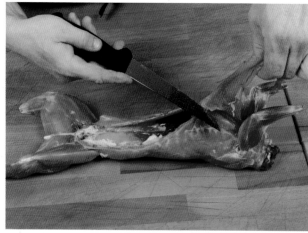

Remove the flanks.

Lay the rabbit on its back and split the rib cage through the sternum.

■ Remove liver, heart and lungs.

1

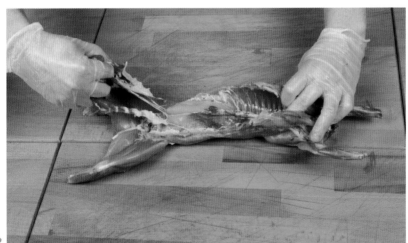

2

3

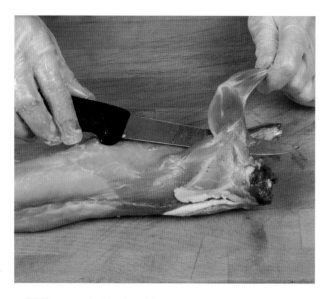

Remove both shoulders.

Cut along the side of each thigh.

Break the thighs backwards to release the bone.

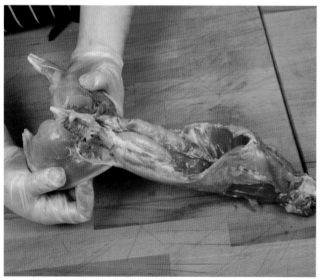

1

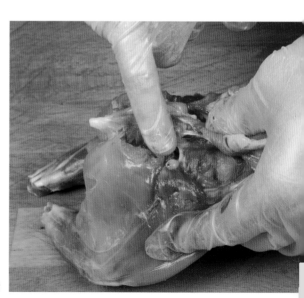

2

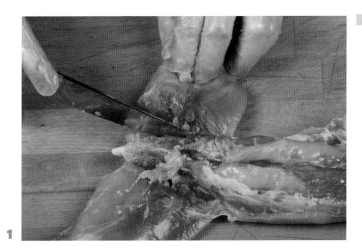

Cut between hip bones and socket to remove the thighs.

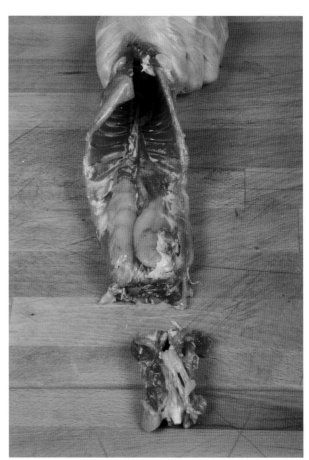

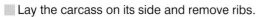With a cleaver, remove the pelvic H-bone.

Lay the carcass on its side and remove ribs.

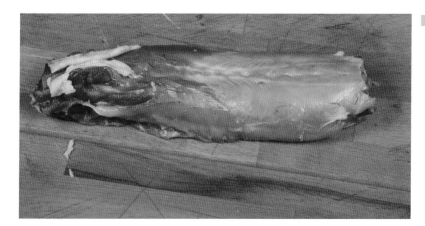
This leaves the long saddle.

Cut through saddle at level of third rib and discard the front end.

Jointed rabbit.

Squirrel

Gutting.

Treat exactly as for a
rabbit as described.
These photographs
illustrate what is
done.

Skinning.

1

2

3

Ready for cooking.

SALMON
AND TROUT

GUTTING FISH

The techniques involved in neatly gutting a fish couldn't be easier.

For a round fish such as a trout or a bass, simply hold the fish upside down, with the head pointing away from you. Insert a sharp pointed knife into the fish's anal vent, then run the blade up until you reach the point of its jaw. Lay the knife down, and grasp the innards at the front end with two fingers. Pull all the guts out with one movement. On a round fish, you also need to remove the dark line of blood along the underside of the spine.

For a small fish like a sardine, make the cut half as long and hook the guts out with one finger.

For flat fish, the guts lie to one side of the body – just cut from the vent as normal and remove.

PREPARATION FOR THE TABLE

Salmon, chopping board, filleting knife.

Insert the knife at centre line just behind the gills. Cut all the way through.

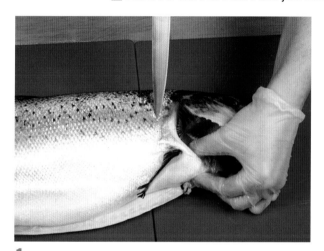

1

2

3

4

Grasp the fish firmly by the gills and continue to cut all the way round the back of its head.

3

4

5

Turn the fish over and repeat the process.

1

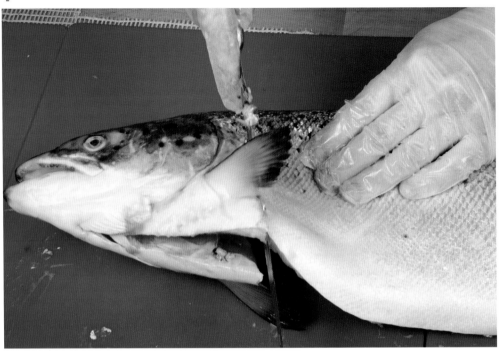

2

5

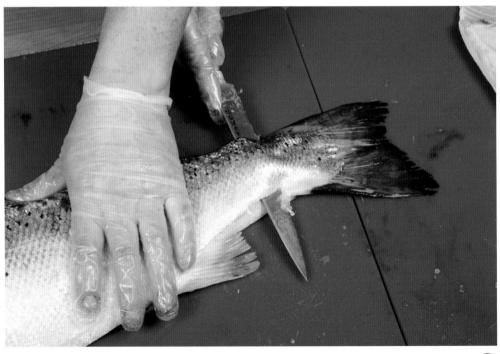

6

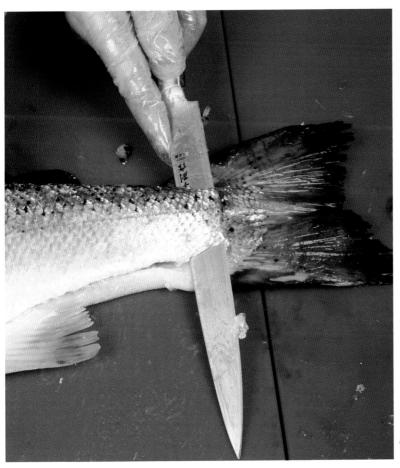

7

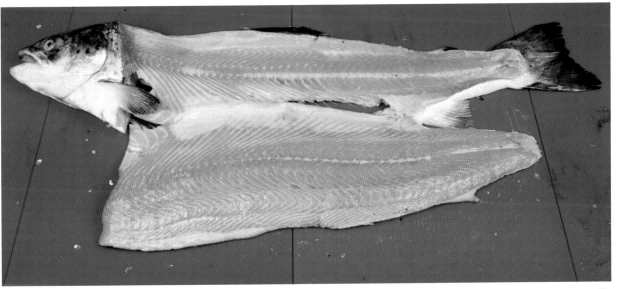

8

Using a shallow cut of the knife, remove the fatty part of the fillet then using fine-nosed pliers, remove the pin bones that run down the centre line of the fillet to about the half way point.

1

2

5

6

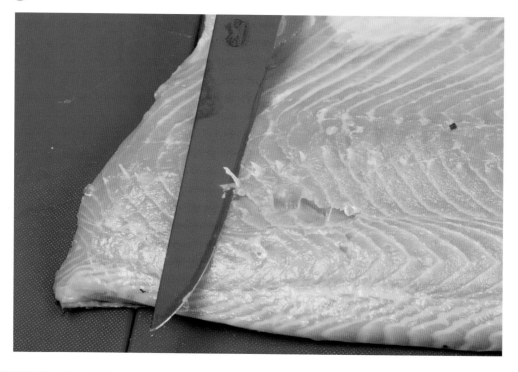

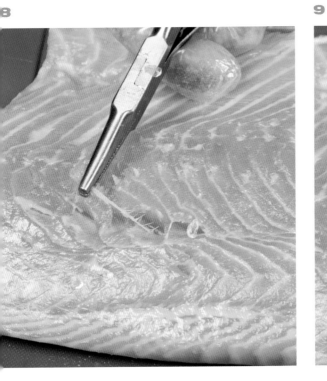

To remove the skin, lay the fillet flat on the board, make a diagonal cut.

1

2

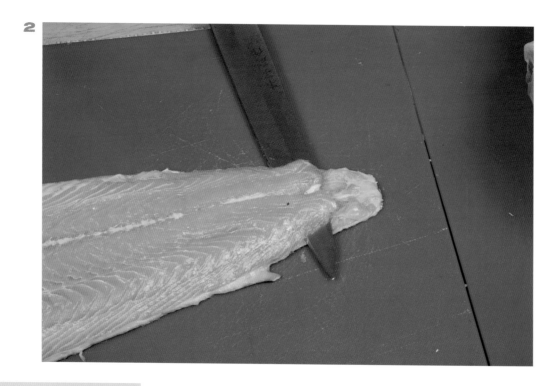

3

4

Grip firmly between thumb and forefinger and slide the knife between skin and flesh.

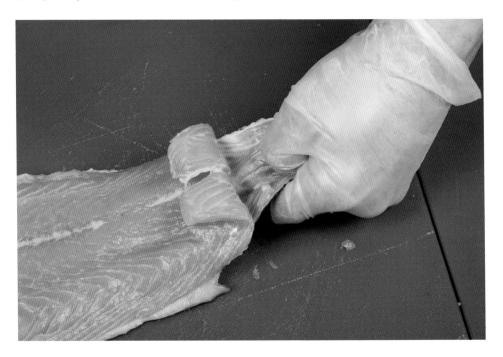

Continue until flesh and skin have separated and the fish is ready for cooking.

An alternative method for trout is shown here.

Slash deeply three or four times on each side and insert slices of lemon into the cuts prior to roasting.

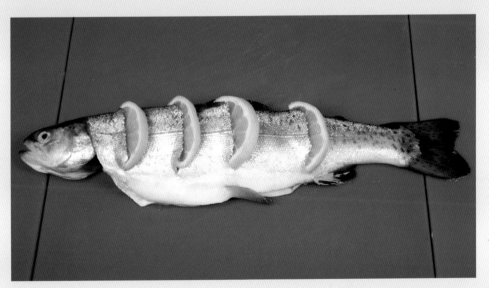

Ready for roasting.